Mountain Gravity

New Atlantic Media
Chapel Hill, NC
2014

Mountain Gravity

[signature: Laurence Avery]

LAURENCE AVERY

Cover design and illustration by Raúl Peña (raulpg.com)
Book design by Raúl Peña (raulpg.com)
Printed in the United States of America

First Printing: February 2014
New Atlantic Media, Chapel Hill, NC
info@newatlanticmedia.org

ISBN 978-0-615-87747-1

Contents

Acknowledgements

Acknowledgements are due to the editors of the following, where some of these poems appeared for the first time: *North Carolina Literary Review*, *Pembroke Magazine*, *Poetry Southeast*, *Sandhills Review*, *Sewanee Review*, *Tar River Poetry*, and *West End Poetry*.

Thanks to a host of friends for their helpful comments on a number of the poems: Cece Conway, Michael Cornett, David Frauenfelder, Hillary Holliday, David Lange, Jennifer Lange, Terri Lange, Lou Lipsitz, Jack Raper, Elizabeth Robinson, Alan Shapiro, and Elizabeth Spencer.

Thanks, too, to Michael McFee, whose encouragement and sympathetic readings have improved my poems for years; and to my cousin, Joe Holder, historian of our clan, whose knowledge of family history, always generously supplied, underlies a number of the poems.

Not on the Nightly News

It's only a copper basin I leveled
with rocks on the ground to let all comers drink,
and nothing like a real pond in the woods
where you'd expect fish to rise
and give unlucky mosquitoes a kiss
or turtles to paddle, only their heads above water
making it hard to tell they aren't snakes,
so we were surprised by the sight. "Look!"
my wife called from the sunroom, "now he's
at the birdbath, hanging over the edge,
head under water, back legs dangling out.
Maybe he's stuck. Will he drown, do you think?"
Our woods, with damp leaf mold, earthworms galore,
scattered ferns and berry tangles —
and far from asphalt with crushing traffic —
make a snug harbor for box turtles,
and the one in our birdbath is not dying.
He lifts his head, urinates over the edge,
and slides in all the way, yellowish shell-splotches
shinning in the sun. We've followed this fellow
all summer, checked for a concave curvature
of his belly shell to learn his gender,
left bits of apple for him to find, and laughed
as he jabbed and snapped at the intruder
he confronts in our reflection ball.
But scrambling into the birdbath, that's new,
and we grab the binoculars. He paddle-crawls
from side to side, stops in the middle to rest,
head in the water, then out to scout about,
sparks flying when the sun strikes his red eyes.
Then he crawls over the edge and drops in a bed
of cinnamon ferns. The swaying spikes
as he lumbers through, I take as a dance
in praise of bombshells whose cost in carnage
is only a few broken fronds.

Celebration

Weeks of sickrooms, then fresh air again —
and celebration along the creek.
Water level on rocks about where it had been
last time I was down here. Same game of hide-and-seek
among squirrels in trees. But poplars now show leafy frills,
not skeletons against the sky; and dogwoods, snowy
petals gone, add their green to the understory.
A puff of crowd roar from a distant stadium fills
the woods with quiet peace. Chirp and chatter
all around feel like a welcome. And low trees are alive
with *bignonia capreolata*, "sweet roving climbers"
Bartram called them in his travels here in 1775,
vines aflame with orange flowers arrayed
like candles in holy places brightening the shade.

Swimming

Triathlete physiques are fine —
clothes hang loose, comfortable,
like granny dresses on matchstick figures,
hiding shoulders, arms, hips, thighs
rounded and rolling with vigor.

At the pool such folks work out from lists,
use lots of paraphernalia — flippers,
hand-paddles, kick-boards, pull-buoys, bottled water —
striving against the clock in more ways than one.

But racing isn't what I'm there for,
and usually I'm content to swim my swim
alone for all the world in a gurgling corridor,
striving to remember how many laps I've done.

Most people approach it much the same,
I think. With something like a prayer
you do a lap or two
to see if all the parts are working right

(that they were the day before means little).
Then you pace yourself to go the distance
and sometimes, finding a groove, notice
with surprise how easily the resistance

of water submits to hips, shoulders
rolling smoothly and staying high.
Those are good days, when you acquire
only some of the aches that mortify.

Afterwards for a little while
there is a feeling of being alive.

Saint Kevin of Glendalough

Seamus the beekeeper saw nothing strange
about Kevin. It is true that in bleak winter
otters brought Kevin a salmon each day,

which the saint blessed and fed to his followers;
but Seamus, perhaps slow of wit, saw only
a small difference between that and his bees,

whose hives nourished the community year-round.
Of course Seamus loved Kevin and was not
wont to find fault, had loved him ever since

that morning he watched Kevin and the angel
walk across the surface of the lake deep
in conversation, the angel saying that

Kevin should build his monastery on the hillside
overlooking the lake and God would honor him
by causing a great city to spring up around it,

and Kevin saying, no, he did not want other
of God's creatures jostled aside on his account,
that all the animals about these mountains

were members of his household and would feel sorrowful
at what the angel proposed. Seamus, no saint,
thought only of his bees and the clover fields

and climbing honeysuckle a city would waste.
But he didn't worry, knowing Kevin meant
what he said. After all, there was that time

with the blackbird. Every day Kevin prayed
on the lake shore, arms flung out like the cross,
palms upturned to heaven. One day as he prayed

a blackbird flew down with a twig, then with another
and another until she had built a nest in his hand,
and in it laid three speckled eggs. Loving the life

in all things, Kevin felt the busy claws and warm
feathery breast and stood still for hours
and days and nights and weeks till the clutch

hatched and fledged and, chirping, flew away.
After this the angel came to visit and bade Kevin
leave off such hard devotion. Kevin said

the pain of holding out his arm like a tree limb
for the blackbird was slight compared
to the pain his Lord suffered for his sake

on the cross. When at last it came time
for Kevin to die, Seamus hoped they would
leave his bones on the hilltop like a stag's

and preserve his spirit instead of his relics.

LEDs?

Acronym, somebody says, for *Light-Emitting Diodes*.

Okay. But *diodes*?

So I parse it: *di* from Greek meaning *two*,
as in carbon *di*oxide. And *odes* —
it pops in my head
that LEDs are a couple of POEMs
paired to emit light —

the last ode in *Oedipus Rex* and "Ode to a Nightingale,"
paired, emit uncommon light
on the slings and arrows of outrageous fortune.

As do the "Intimations" ode and the one "on the Death
of a Favourite Cat" on the urge
to gather ye rose-buds while ye may.

But then matter-of-fact glares in
to disentangle *enlightenment* and *luminosity*
with something about semiconductors and two *paths*
(Greek root again) for electrical currents.
Unlike halogen, fluorescent, and incandescent,
LEDs are tiny, long-lasting, and efficient —
a rising star on the green horizon.

The prospect seems about as bright as such things get
that LEDs will go easy on the planet and your purse,
and make a better light for reading odes.

Birdbath

Birdbath, I used to think,
was the mistaken name of a place
where birds get a drink — a mistake
betraying the lure of alliteration.
Bird drinking place has no ring to it,
you'll agree. But now I know
it's no mistake. Birds must bathe
to tend their feathers and do so elaborately
(with alliterations, being true
is no big drawback).

Clowns of the backyard garden
are boat-tailed grackles
(*paddle*-tailed grackle is more like it
but trips up the tongue in the speaking).
Swarming the bath, they flop in three and four at a time
for a flutter that showers the flowers,
then rise to fill the trees with crazy chatter.

Small birds, watching a chance,
dart in for a dip and zip away,
understating their presence as minor characters do.

Doves are invisible grazing toward the water
on faded brown leaves in the shadows
until a bobbing head calls attention
or one of their number, neck arched,
feathers distended, puts on a rush
to bully a squirrel. (These truculent birds
symbolize peace for their beautiful lines,
all gentle curves, but that only proves
the power of form — and nobody bothered
to tell *them* about it.) At the bath
they drink like you and me,

not throwing back their head to swallow,
then step in, flutter a time or two,
and for an instant,
preening serenely in the sun,
shimmer in pinks and greens about the neck
before feathers flatten, and they fade again
into the brown leaves and shadows.

But any piece about baths
is really about another bird. Robins
are the epic bathers — *Sing through me, Muse,*
of the… But what muse will do here?
O Fiacre, guardian of gardens
sing through me of the birdbath bombast
of that bumptious bird, grandest of all
garden bathers from rose-fingered… — Well,
a little of the high style goes a long way.
But day after day the robins come,
and when they arrive, take over.

One is in the water now,
an old friend of mine. Plunge and flutter,
plunge and flutter — he has been at it
a while already.

I can tell you how the thing began.
An hour ago, hose and scrub brush in hand,
I hauled myself out to clean the bath.
Everybody scattered — birds, squirrels,
mosquitoes — all but this fellow.
Defiant, he hopped not a stone's throw away
and stalked about, gobbling earthworms
with resentful vigor, keeping one eye always on me.

I wasn't back to the house before
there he was again in the clean clear water,
where he is now, dousing himself and fluttering,
and every now and again sweeping
his kingdom with a commanding glare.
He's the best acrobat of the bunch.
I'll swear he balances on his beak when,
rump and feet to the sky, he plunges under.

What but hubris can account for the looming fall —
if hubris govern in a thing so small —
when this cocky fellow flies off with soggy feathers
and rises, not like a hawk on mighty wings,
or an eagle soaring, but like a goose
who labors skyward with a rising motion
suggestive of sinking.

Mountain Gravity

Up here at five thousand feet, crests
of the Blue Ridge roll away as far
as you can see — green, blue,
smoky gray. On the Parkway,
riding the ridges along old hunting trails,
you look down through patches of mist
to coves and hollows once peopled by my ancestors,
some who swapped the wide sky of Connecticut
for the narrow skies of these mountain valleys,
others who grew corn here and hunted deer
long before de Soto trampled through.
I've come to hike the valley below me,
now a mixed oak forest where last year
the screech of sneakers in a gym
coming from a dead treetop gave me
my first good look at a rose-breasted grosbeak
calling in his brood at dusk.

— Along the creek that drains the high valley,
birds and butterflies dodge among green leaves
heedless of the man hunched on a rock
watching the water splash down
stair-step falls and run on, always down
toward larger streams — French Broad, Tennessee,
Mississippi — back to its source in the Gulf.

II

As if She Listened

for my great-grandmother

I have seen her only in faded family photos
        seated by her husband,
        flanked by five grown sons,

all posing in the dirt farmyard. Her sons,
        stiff and unsmiling,
        strive to look their manly part.

Her husband (starched collar, dark suit, long string tie
        like the boys)
        scowls at the camera

as if suddenly doubtful a family portrait is worth
        a missed hour of plowing.
        While he strains forward,

she sits back, tilting her chair, long fingers
        spread on her lap,
        looking comfortable,

the hint of a smile on her lips at the draped tri-pod contraption
        hauled up from the town
        below in the valley.

She's in Victorian dress (high neck, long sleeves,
        wide skirt down to the ground)
        designed to cancel

the female body, but rivercane baskets scattered behind her
        on the porch
        conjure her for me —

a woman's work-baskets for gathering corn, sifting meal,
       the nurturing chores —
       a woman

who took the hand of a white farmer in the Blue Ridge foothills
       in the dwindling days of her tribe,
       yet watched the white world

around her as from a distance, as if she listened
       to the nosy wrens
       along the Oconaluftee

who sang the spirit of the Cherokees when babies arrived
       in the mountain towns
       of her people,

mournful songs when the child was a boy — *Alas! the whistle of arrows!* —
       but joyful
       when the gift was a girl —

All thanks! the pounding of corn in a hollowed stump,
       the swish
       of sifters!

Letter from Nanye'hi,
Beloved Woman of the Cherokees,
to Benjamin Franklin, Governor of Pennsylvania
(September 1787)

Brother, not long ago I bounced over
the Appalachians on a horse that jolted
my old bones into one big ache,
then hobbled to a barge that soaked my pack,
making my way to your flat city near the water side,
all in the service of peace between our people.
Two years ago — I heard you were in France —
we gave up our rolling woodlands east of the Blue Ridge.
In exchange, your Continental Congress promised
to protect us in our mountains and lands westward
through the Cumberland country. *Hopewell*,
the treaty was called, our first with your new government.
But we have had not one day of peace,
and our hope vanishes like morning mist
in the growing light of day. Every week
more settlers arrive, and like unruly children
lay hands on our land for farm or settlement;
and your government, a negligent parent,
does nothing to prevent their coming or make them behave.
Hotheads, both red and white, have no trouble
resorting to bullets, fire, and knives.
Retaliation follows reprisal follows retribution —
a bloody cycle I hoped to stop
by visiting your Congress in Philadelphia,
a name I love for what it means.

My talk was this: *Sirs, woman does not*
pick babies from bushes or pull them from hollow logs,
but out of her own body. She gives life to all,
and all should look on her as a mother
and mind what she says. I look on the settlers as my children,
along with the red people. You have heard how I freed

a settler kidnapped from her home and already tied
to the stake for burning, my warriors dancing around.
And I warn settlers of surprise attacks
by vengeful Cherokees. "That is no way to behave
toward our sisters and brothers," I tell my warriors.
"Treat them like kin and help them see the light."
Sometimes the warriors heed my words. I have come now
to keep the path straight and clear between us,
and to see whether you have among your people
a Beloved Woman who feels for all her children,
red as well as white, and can speak to
your unruly children in my homeland
as I speak to my young warriors. I see no women
in your council today. That would not happen in my towns.
Do you have such a woman as I speak of?
I hope you do. This message comes
from the bottom of my heart. We want to live in peace.

Brother, that was my talk, yet back home
I was not off my horse before hearing
that things had gone from bad to worse.
The settlers, now styling themselves the State of Franklin,
sent word that North Carolina had given them
the Cumberland country, and they intend
to take it from the Cherokees "by the sword,
which is the best right to all countries."
Imagine that! Our territory is no more
North Carolina's to give than my shawl is!
And might can't make a thing right, even for white men.
Where is the American government we trusted
when we made the Hopewell treaty? Why doesn't
it step in and make its children leave us in peace?

That is the reason I write to you.
I know you respect the red people of the land.
Even in the early days you commended
the Iroquois Confederation on its plan of government.

And among your own people not even General Washington
stands in higher esteem than you. You also know
a thing or two about treaties, having negotiated a few.
Can you not persuade your Congress to enforce our treaty,
even "by the sword," if need be, and compel the squatters
to live in peace with us?

Brother, you and I are old,
and soon will leave the problems of the world
to our children. They will have enough of them,
without these troubles between our two peoples.
Do what you can. I am growing tired . . . . — but, oh,
do you love orchards as I do?
There is an orchard on the hill behind my house,
and come June, whole days when I swear
I could place all the squabbling children
where a breeze off the lake startles the apple blossoms
and negotiate a lasting peace!

GRANDDAD
for W. H. A.
Memoria in aeterna

1. His Home

The mountain waited for someone with vision.
Many had traveled the valley below;
the setting had caught the eye of none.
As soon as he saw it, his eyes glowed.

The ridge rose sharply from the valley floor
with halfway up a level lap of land,
then rose again in towering encore.
For a home, the site was grand.

Other young men with families rented.
He worked nights as a factory warden
to earn a down payment on 200 acres.
Cherokees before him had hunted the mountain.

Other men opted for the easy way out,
built close to the road, left the house unpainted.
A mile up it was to the lap where he built —
he didn't move in till the house was painted.

White! The sight made travelers stop
and stare, hooked as by a harvest moon.
From his porch the valley view lifted you up.
The mountain had waited for someone with vision.

2. His Books

lined two walls of the room, English
on one wall, Latin on the other. A Latin teacher
turned farmer as the AEF boys shipped out for France
to make the world safe for democracy,
he needed books like he needed bread.
"My inspiration for a time," he told me once
when, as a kid, I picked up his worn copy
of the *Georgics*. "Farming from seeds to bees.
Of course, not much there about tractors."
He winked, but I had missed the joke,
not knowing then when the *Georgics* were written.

My favorite came from the other wall,
an illustrated tales of Sherwood Forest.
Robin and his Merry Men
whack the wicked, back the good.
Slip into Nottingham disguised as beggars,
with longbow best the best of the sheriff's archers.

But at night, grandparents off in the kitchen
beyond the room where the cats slept,
I would stumble on the wrong pictures.
The puddle of light from a kerosene lamp
left me engulfed in the dark. If I even twitched,
bright eyes glinted through the doorway, fierce, unblinking.
Around a Sherwood Forest oak,
a grim face glared as at its next victim.
Gnarly tree roots half out of the ground
crawled my way like mountain rattlers.

3. His Friend

Off-days at the CCC camp, John Robert
sometimes ate at grandmother's table.
One Saturday, out hunting, he stopped by.

"Whar's your grandpaw, tyke?" he asked me in the yard.
"I got me a rale problem. I mislike
 being a bother, but I need to see Mister William."

Rifle barrel resting on the toe of his shoe,
he went rambling on — "Bet you hern of pelicans,
but bet you don't know they . . ." — until, *bam!*

"Lord 'a mercy! Done shot myself in the foot!"
He was on the ground when Granddad ran out,
 got off the bloody shoe, raised his foot above heart level.

"It'll help control the bleeding," he told
 a puzzled John. "I'll clean the wound, get you
 in the car and back to camp for medical care."

"But Mister William, I got me a rale problem.
'T'ain't nothing to do with no foot. My gu'ment pay,
 hit's thirty a month, me to keep five, send twenty-five

back to the folks — back to something I ain't got!
I sho' don't want to get charged with no felony!"
Granddad said, "Once I get you in the medical tent

I'll speak to the camp commander.
He'll have it in his files that you were orphaned
as a child. Now let's ride."

4. His Day In Court

Neighborhood boys butchered one of granddad's heifers
and took the meat to market for thirty-seven dollars,
then drunk at a dance bragged of the deed in the presence
of a grand juror. At their trial granddad
spoke briefly with the judge and left.

"The heifer was his,
Mr. Avery says, but he won't press charges,
preferring good will among neighbors to righting a wrong."

The judge glared. "By god, boys, you've played the fool,
but it lets you see how a good man thinks!"

Laughing later my uncle recalled the theft.
"When the old barn burned, those boys worked
from sun to sun till the thing was rebuilt.
Thirty-seven bucks? We made money on their guilt!"

5. His Wedding Photo

Old photo in hand, I sit on the deck at dusk
listening as I often do to the brusque
notes of a cardinal high in an oak as he calls
his brood to collect for the night. The photo shows
my granddad on his wedding day, trying to look composed
but failing — anxious rather, as if in free-fall.

But the granddad I knew never fretted in doubt.
Sure of himself he was, independent without
being cold. His gaze I remember as bemused but steady.
At six I uprooted a lilac bush in his yard.
"Oh my!" grandmother lamented, taking it hard.
His remark: "If that boy did it, it was dead already."

The world was not a mystery to my granddad.
One night, sons complaining on the porch how bad
things were, how inflation was driving them insane,
how the world was going to hell in a handbasket — he broke in:
"In twenty-two my first Ford car cost five bales of cotton.
Nothing's changed. The one I have now cost about the same."

My glass empty, I think of going in,
but the cardinal, calling still, calls back my kin.
One summer, air rifle in tow, I terrorized grove and creek
till granddad took me aside and gave me a warning:
"You know that mockingbird I listen to of a morning?
Mind, then, shoot it and I'll wring your neck."

Like most old photos, mine will wind up stashed someplace
to crack and fade. But the puzzled young face,
not half my present age, amplifies and brightens
the man I knew years later — and conveys
a true sense after all. On your wedding day
it is only rightful to look uncertain.

A Lass and the Ethnographer
(QUALLA BOUNDARY, NORTH CAROLINA, SUMMER 1887)
for my great-grandmother

The application of their herbal medicines was not the whole, and in fact was rather the subordinate, part of the Cherokee treatment of illnesses, which was always accompanied by certain ceremonies and "words." These are the sacred formulas of the Cherokees — their prayers, songs, prescriptions, charms, and spells... A lass gifted with a ready comprehension had some knowledge of the formulas and volunteered to write out the words for me in English, but failed to do so at first, owing chiefly to the opposition of the shamans.

James Mooney, *Sacred Formulas of the Cherokees*

He was astonished "a lass"
knew the formulas of the shamans,
could translate from Cherokee to English with ease,
was bold enough to step up and volunteer —
that most of all.
I enjoyed his surprise,
fancied myself the more for his dismay
that Cherokee women are not like women in his towns,
who cover themselves from neck to toe
like they are ashamed of their bodies,
and are always deferential in public,
as if men count for more in life's balance.
That is not the Cherokee way.

But it's true,
after volunteering to translate the formulas,
I hesitated before the shamans.
They came to me with scowls and said, if I
revealed anything to our visitor, he would take
the information to Washington and lock it in a box,
and we would lose the use of it.

You mustn't laugh at that foolish notion.
Frightened people don't show at their best.
I watch the shamans at dusk wander into the mist off the Oconaluftee,
their blue bandanas the last thing you see —
blue, our color for despair —
and their eyes are turned inward
to the mountains and towns long ago
when their formulas seemed powerful to everyone
and the shamans were indispensable to the whole people.
Now we all take aspirin from the dispensary for a headache,
not a pennyroyal poultice and a secret chant —
all but the oldest among us.

That got me to thinking.
Our yesterdays pile up like dry leaves in the fall
and are blowing away as I watch.
But I want to be remembered —
my day remembered, and the days of my mother and grandmothers,
who suffered far worse at the hands of the whites
in the time of the removal, and before.
But how can our children remember, and our grandchildren,
if they have no glimpse of us,
if the old days have blown away like dry leaves?

I dream in white,
color of happiness and peace among us (odd as that is, now) —
nice sheets, twilight, snow-covered hemlocks.
But I dress in red,
our color for triumph.
So I sat down to work.
The translations will preserve our knowledge for the future,
and for them Mr. Mooney promises me
he will ease the days of the shamans with greenbacks.

Sgê! Listen to me, James Mooney!
In these formulas I have sprinkled seven mistakes —
a powerful number that muddles their meaning,
and I will mend the mistakes
only when I see you keep your promise to my people!

III

Mysteries

Who knows how a child learns what trees are?
With infants, things must strike the brain
like boats in a fog, or shooting stars —
stray pieces from missing puzzles.
And who recalls when it dawned on them
that to get fed you cry, that you might stand upright
if you try, or when in the babble a word takes shape
like a pebble in a stream? But along the way old heads
go to some trouble –"Tree, that's a tree" —
and grow excited too when a child in the woods
starts turning and pointing, "tree, tree," until she
falls down laughing, "I want to do it again and again
and again!" In no time she asks, eyes intent, busy:
"That tree over there, what kind is he?"

Steps

That one purrs till she pulls its tail. Then it bites
her hand and runs away on all fours, like her —
but the motion jangles, the rhythm not right.
And now it's scary: her hand still hurts.

The others, towering way above, move
differently. She's been watching. She can't dance
to the tune they dance to, but the beat of their music
calls out to her. Its rhythm makes sense.

They stand up straight like her bottle on the table.
Getting feet under, she pulls up, lets go, and stands
like a bottle. Then lifts a foot and, with forward wobble,
sets it down, for balance waggling outheld hands.

If months turn to years in the normal way,
other steps will follow.

Hop-scotch skipping will soon make a beat
for "Dad, look at me!"

Her teens will rankle like a sonata
with a sprinkle of wrong notes.

In time, she'll find a song she wants to sing
because it suits her.

By then, the rhythm of her ways
will show in all she does.

Practicing, she'll perform herself
in the way she sits, hands poised to play.

But now, hands held out for balance,
she takes it a step at a time, pausing
on each foot to test the feel before advancing.

This mode of locomotion is hard,
the rhythm herky-jerky,
but no later steps will feel so good.

It's a moment of debut.
Bright eyes shout the thrill:
"Hey look! It's me! And I am one of you!"

A Grip on Things

He couldn't have been more than four,
in the dressing room by himself
probably the first time.
Finished with the business
that brought him in from the pool,
he hopped about
tugging this way and that
in an effort doomed by the fact
that nothing beats a wet bathing suit
in the number of ways
it can turn wrong-side out.
Everything still at half-mast,
he paused, shoulders slumping.

Then his face firmed up
as he went back to work,
announcing to the room at large:
"It's all right to be naked in here.
It's not all right to be naked out there."

Through a Glass Darkly

In my Radio Flyer we shoot down the hill,
me squeezed between her knees gripping the handle,
her digging ten fingers in my shoulders,
our future looking fuzzy from the wind in our faces,

both of us shouting, *Hold on!*

When the Flyer comes to rest, we race
to the creek as always and try skipping stones on the water.
I make one bounce three times and feel like king for a day,
but she gets a flatter one to take four hops, then says,

I bet you can't even pull me for a ride in the creek.

She's finished fifth grade, I only the second,
but she's not much bigger than me,
and the water just comes to my knees,
and her uppity tone right out of the blue gets my goat,

and I say, *Yes, I can.*

We're well out in the current —
she sits on her knees looking at me funny,
as if she's never seen me before
(we've only played together all my life!) —

when the big kid down the street wades in behind us.

You'd think she's used her mother's make-up,
her cheeks get so red.
Then laughing, she swings bare legs out the back
and kicks up water all over his front.

You better stop, he calls,

but he is laughing, too,
and scoops up a handful of pebbles
and lobs them in her direction,
and she says,

You better sto-op.

They are laughing and splashing and tossing
and making my job well neigh impossible.
Her swinging legs get the wagon to lurching,
and I stumble backwards plop in the water.

Why don't they open their eyes?

I wonder in drenched consternation.
Either she should get out,
or he should help me pull.
It's as simple as that.

It floors me they can't see what's going on!

An Early Rorschach

I remember the road down the valley,
on one hand a pasture fence at the foot of a hill,
on the other a field of green corn higher than my head.
Walking the road I would keep an eye on the fence
for blackberries and places granddad's cows
might get out. But one bright noon a black snake
caught my eye in the road up ahead racing
toward me in the dust, or seeming to
in the heat shimmer. I scrambled off the road
and up the bank through brambles and barbed wire —
then forgot snakes and scratches. Up there
what I saw across the road beyond the corn
was a mountain ridge against the sky
with trees in the shape of a woman running by.

Red Shoes

These days you must learn to walk again,
and not in shoes like those your mother gave you
as soon as you could scoot without scuffing the toes —
gleaming red with silver buckles. Those springtime days
you skipped out and paraded on the lawn so passersby
could admire your patent leather treasures,
and at night your heart said the red glow in the sky
above steel mill furnaces came from your red shoes.

In these autumn days your shoes are only
trimmed in red, one lined with carbon-fiber —
the bones of a foot shattered by a spill from a ladder.
Now baths in a cast, stairs in the wheel chair's path,
tempt tears. A walking-boot, like endless
cobblestones, jolts every joint. To parade
again, you must listen to your heart once more.
Amica mea, this time you dare not wait for the dark.

IV

Planting Time
(after W. B. Yeats)

We sat together one spring evening,
you and I, and talked as people do
of this and that. You said: "Finally,
everything is in the ground!
All we spent the winter hunting for —
ferns, hostas, hellebores beneath
the trees; along the edges ginger, sweet woodruff,
plumbago — awful name, suggests disease,
but all the same among my new delights
for its little hanging flowers, cornflower blue
and new each morning. I worried, when we couldn't
steal the time to dig, that summer would come
and find us planting still. Heat
could do it all in before the roots
take hold. Then where would we be? But we beat the days
when the sun shines hot — mosquitoes too."

"You dug all day and so did I," I said.
"Classrooms are gardens, only it's rare
you see much growth, even when you've labored.
Often you're tempted to say that teaching
would be a great job if it weren't for the students.
Today, though, a fellow declared in class
that at the airport with an hour to kill
he looked for a sports mag on the racks,
but spotting Tennyson's *Idylls of the King*,
picked it up instead. Smile if you like,
that's news to brighten a rainy day:
verse tale, one; sports mag, zero."

In dusk's white light we watched the new-leafed oaks
grow distinct against the sky
and begin to sway as a breeze came up
like dancers more than pleased
to find a rhythm working them —
revived, gladdened in the moment.
Tags for names were the final thing.
You handed me one and started another
while I found the plant, parted its foliage,
and pushed the stake down low. After a while,
the naming done, we turned to go
as the evening star grew bright.
You were amazed how the time had flown,
and I thought we'd been surprised by a visitation
like the dancing trees.

Goldfinches In A Patch
of Coneflowers

Perching lightly at the tip-top
on cones with rosé petals, birds dine
on seeds and sips of dewdrop,

swaying with the rhythm of the breeze;
drift down as stalks give way in gentle arc,
then from low in green leaves

shoot up in yellow spurts and whistle
a lilting fol-de-rol before sailing back
to sport a heartbeat at the very pinnacle.

Mulberries

Mother Goose to the contrary notwithstanding,
the mulberries in my woods are trees, not bushes,
with berries that are juicy, crunchy, and tart.

Much of the harvest, of course, is filched by the critters.
Some folks, robbed of their labor on trees they fertilize,
water, and prune, would feel put out.
But there are other pleasures than eating,
and I've come to consider the mulberries a spectator sport.

With berries dangling under limbs on long slender stems,
you'd think they were out of reach for birds and squirrels.
I am no lover of squirrels. Their depredations
on everything — plants, birdfeeders, garden furniture —
are enough to exasperate the mildest gardener.
For all their agility, they are mindless creatures,
half the time burying acorns, the other half
forgetting where and digging up, say,
a maidenhair fern, as if it might have sprung
from one. I stop far short of admiration
when I see a squirrel in the mulberries
slung under a limb by all fours and shinnying along,
the berries now at mouth level and disappearing fast.
I can stand the sight only so long,
and pretty soon shoo the rascal off
(only to watch as he throws himself at a birdfeeder).

Birds, on the other hand — swimmers in the air —
I could watch all day. In the mulberries it's the usual
backyard crowd: mockers, catbirds, and thrashers
of the amazing *arias d'imitazione*; raucous crows and jays;
flashy goldfinch, cardinals, and rufous-sided towhees;
purple grackles and assorted sparrows; little titmice,
chickadees, and wrens; even insectivorous
bluebirds, flickers, and red-bellied woodpeckers
along with ground-feeding doves and robins.
All these flock and flutter around the trees
during mulberry season. In late May
when green sour lumps appear, birds stop by
every day like kids eyeing cookies in the oven.
By early June some pink shows, and interest
grows intense. Soon the leafy trees are aboil
with birds chirping, squawking, chasing, returning.

In the end no bird gets many berries.
Could they swing under a limb like squirrels,
it would be a different story. As it is,
they busy themselves atop a limb
two-stepping this way and that as they crane
to reach a berry over-head — with little success
since pruning keeps branches well spaced.

No bird, that is, but one. With robins
it *is* a different story. They crane and two-step too,
but are looking for a ripe berry several feet off,
then guided missile-like, launch themselves at it,
snatch the berry in flight, land to gobble it down,
and go back for more.

Sound easy? Few birds attempt it,
even after robins show them how,
and those that try mess up the fly-by big time.
I watched a jay, after six or eight misses,
plough into a limb and, dazed, give it up.
It occurs only with robins — the body control,
timing, and what we'd call digital dexterity
were it done with fingers instead of a beak.

Their exploits are a benefaction.
Watching them, my spirit lifts as it always does
at the graceful execution of a well-imagined action.

For Gilbert White,
Out-Door Naturalist of Selborne
(1720-1793)

Just above the trees this morning
a dozen pigeons cut tight figure-eights
for half an hour, wheeling and swooping together
like dancers carefully choreographed,
then on cue flew off south.
I hadn't seen such an aerial ballet before
and watched intrigued by so much play
unrelated to eating or breeding. I wonder
if you ever saw such a sight, Mr. White? Not likely.
At least it doesn't appear in those letters you wrote,
so meticulous they tell us which birds walk, which hop.
Still, my pigeons find shelter under your nudging principle:
"all nature is so full, that that district produces
the greatest variety which is the most examined."

Rainy Nights

My fingers trace the curve of her hip;
she stirs, moves closer, without waking.
Light rain in trees out the window, delaying dawn,
lulls me back toward sleep
                        and I drift
into another night years ago
when we threw off our shoes and ran out,
delighting in a drought-breaking downpour
that saved our garden: a garden that showed
how it would look if plants that grow under trees
in the Carolina piedmont — arching, ground-hugging,
or bushy; speckled, splotched, or solid;
and green, green, or green —
just happened to spring up in one small woods,
in the right proportions, in neat alignment
with paths, birdbaths, stone and metal figures.
The little girls next door decided
fairies must live in our woods and brought us
two tiny chairs to sit by a low birdbath.
Grownups seeing the garden caught their breath,
and I told them, *it's exhibit A*
of what she can do.
                        I ease out of bed
and move toward the kitchen.
Her mind still races with possibilities.
For the rest, just getting dressed is painful,
and even good days aren't easy.
The rain picks up as I make coffee.
When she comes down,
we can listen to the thrumming on the roof
and smile over the night another downpour
brought us pleasure.

Through the day she'll *take pains*
in several senses of the phrase,
and I'll recall her Christmas amaryllis,
spectacular while its burnt orange flowers lasted,
beautiful in a quieter way
when it featured the clean lines of arching leaves.

November Afternoon

Metabolism accelerates in the cold,
else birds freeze. I fill the feeder
and expect them to be at least a little bold,
by necessity, in pecking at the seeds.

A titmouse and finch alight to feast, but stay
only a second. A gust of wind and both
fly off, frightened by a falling leaf they
mistake for a jay or some other bully.

Safe is better than sorry, for sure, but bold,
at least a little, is what I expect of me.
I'll rhyme to warm my spirits against the cold
and hope to tell the difference between jays and leaves.

Conjuring Tricks

Looking out at our woods, you would notice
a distant roofline through the trees, but I
rarely see it. Ages ago I wheeled in flagstones,
and Rachel, on her knees, fit and leveled them
into walks adopted quickly, to our smiling surprise,
by foxes cruising the woods at dusk. Three spurs
went out to birdbaths, copper basins steadied
with rocks on the ground, and we found before long
we'd fashioned a place where even turtles could drink.
All along we made a game of finding plants
that love the shade — losing often. But we hit
a winner with *arum italicum*, contrarian of the plant world
that sprouts in the fall, sports emerald leaves all winter
over snow or brown leaf-mold, then dies in the spring,
leaving pencil-stalks with berries that ripen bright orange.
Catbirds think we grow the arum for them, and repay us
promptly, dropping seeds wherever they perch.
Now, stray arum in the woods, plants and paths
and baths, conjure a world for me that you won't see.

The Late Display of Yellow Sage

March frosts at daybreak.
Forsythia and quince catch the eye.
In biting air, sage might be lost,
first shoots waving like small hands raised.

Summer sizzle. Goat's beard droops.
Hydrangea sparkles till dry weather, then folds its tent.
Leaves like big shoulders, sage lifts any group —
low greenery on wooded path, ferns under trees.

November twilight. Against all the browns,
whorls of yellow flowers
atop the sage. I tip my cap,
craving the likes of its late display of powers.

V

Dealing with It

"Used to, I could fix
damn near anything"—
a prolix uncle, off of politics
for a change, was holding forth
following my mother's funeral.

"Back when your mom and I came along,
you didn't buy a heck of a lot.
No hi-fis, tvs, highfalutin stuff.
Most everything was foolproof:
churns, wood stoves, kerosene lamps,
sewing machines you pedal,
mops to clean the floor,
a well and a bucket —
something like that breaks,
you chuck it,
or tinker till it works again.

"Nowadays it's a damn sight different.
Say your washer/dryer breaks,
you gotta call Des Moines
to get a number in Atlanta
for 'em to fax somebody over
from Santa Fe to fix it.
You can stay sane living like that,
even be entertained,
as long as you appreciate
how many folks got jobs
rejuvenatin' the stuff —
and have a washpot to use
while you wait."

Shady Oaks

Under the oaks I spoke with the man who ran
the place — an open-air crafts shop in the last bit of woods
along the tourist strip from Panama City
to the beaches. I grew up here, but hadn't been back
to the old home town in decades and was getting glum
over the man-made clutter that hid the blue sky, white sand,
and green water. I mentioned that his shade beat hell
out of the glare along the highway.

"And usually there's a breeze in here under the live oaks.
The old house over there where I have my office,
it gets hot. Built in the eighteen-eighties —
just a shack, but one of the early homes
on Saint Andrews Bay. My partner's in a/c,
says he'd air condition it this minute, says it would help
my business, but I'm not interested,
would change the character of the place.
With a house like that, you open windows."

I went in to pay for the bird house I liked
(some grand hotels were swinging in the trees, but mine
was a single-family dwelling carved from a cypress knee)
and met a cat sprawled on the counter.

"He's on break, you can tell. He has a job,
looking after chickens, but in hot weather
you have to be careful not to over-do it.

"The chickens are pets. Years ago a crate
bounced off a truck and filled the woods
with noisy poultry. I put out grain and water,
added exotics I got from a dealer, and now
have this flock with feathers right down to their feet.

You must have seen them scratching under the display tables —
the chickens scratching, not you. When I was a kid
this place was a farm, so chickens feel right at home.
But hawks are back, started nesting all around the bay,
and like nothing better than a dinner of chicken.
That's why I got me two cats — the other one
out on patrol right now, no doubt."

While he fooled with my charge card, I read a chalkboard
over his shoulder giving dates, times, and places
for a shape-note gospel sing, a showing
of somebody's paintings, a neighborhood farmers' market,
and a class for people new to digital cameras.
The scrawl was a treat. So far I'd seen nothing
but splashy billboards and flashy neon lights —
the native plants of resort towns.

He came back with my sales slip. "How 'bout a beer?
I'm not air conditioned, but I keep a cold keg
for paying customers." While we drank,
I asked if he had a web site.

"Sure do. And after Christmas, it could be
all that's left. The old man I leased from
died last winter. He was my protector —
from an old family on the bay,
liked the way I look at things.
But I just paid his taxes."

I asked the owner's name, recognized it,
and wondered if his heirs had been in touch,
one of whom I knew.

"Not yet, and who knows what they'll do?
They're scattered, and they need money too.
I hope they don't sell. I hate to think about
the old house and the chickens, if this green island
gets swamped by the ocean of asphalt rising around here.
Myself, I can always manage.
Anything you can mail, you can sell on the internet,
and that's most of my stuff. The locals I sell for,
some of 'em barely get by as it is.
Whatever happens, I mean to pick up sales,
attract wholesale business.
Evolve or disappear is my motto.
But here," he handed me a business card —
old house under oaks, contact information at the bottom —
"we can't let this green island go under.
Bet you wouldn't mind putting in a word for me
wherever you can."

Someplace Else

(with apologies to Milne and Dickinson)

Halfway up the mountain
is a place
where she sits.
There isn't another place
quite like it.

Halfway up the mountain
isn't up,
you know,
where everybody
wants to go.

Halfway down the mountain
isn't down
in the town
where everybody
is busy.

All sorts
of funny thoughts
run round her head
when she's not up or down,
but someplace else instead:

"I'm Nobody! Who are you?
Are you — Nobody — too?
Then there's a pair of us!
Don't tell! they'd banish us — you
know!

"How dreary — to be — Somebody!
How public — like a Frog —
To tell your name — the livelong June —
To an admiring Bog!"

73

Puttin' on the Ritz

As soon as the nurses let go her arms,
she flung the walker across the room,
and they had to catch her from falling.
"I'm not using that thing!"
she spluttered, breathing hard.
In her head a picture show was playing
of poor Pete McGowan up the street at home
who was old and decrepit and used a walker.
"I take casseroles to people who use walkers!"

"Physical therapy!" —
the surgeon sounded oracular.
His knife had traumatized her spinal nerves,
and he needed to deflect attention.
"A determined effort at walking —
a not uncommon regimen!"

With the therapists she was always ill tempered,
always adamant in refusing the walker.
A fall brought stitches over one eye.
After three days the hospital gave up
and discharged her.

Back home, inside her house,
the walker got exercised incessantly.
When hubby joked about the path
she would wear in the carpet, she exploded,
"the darn thing hurts my hands and ties them up
and makes my shoulders ache!" —
and kept on clumping.

But let neighbors drop in,
she was sure to be stranded in a chair,
the walker nowhere to be seen. Unless hubby
was handy, visitors had to let themselves out.

In her head a picture show began to play
of Planters' Mr. Peanut and the Monopoly Man,
elegant strutters with top hat and cane.
"Drive me to the drugstore," she told hubby,
and went in on his arm
and bought a walking stick.

And there she was on a stroll
up the sidewalk to the McGowan house,
hubby bearing the casserole.
A song was playing in her head:
*Come, let's mix where Rockefellers walk with sticks and um-ber-ellas
in their mitts —*
Puttin' on...

Smiling at the way she swayed and flourished the cane,
neighbors marveled at how steady she was on her feet,
how almost normal in her stride —
though on a second look
they noticed too how slowly she moved.

Meanwhile, the song flowering into living Technicolor,
she danced on up the street with Fred Astaire,
herself the glittering glamorous gorgeous blond
puttin' on the Ritz.

Driving in England

At the car rental place in Windermere
I told the woman my only worry was that
drivers over here might sit on the side called right,
but for sure they drive on the wrong side of the street.
"How can it be wrong when it's the side your heart is on?"
she chirped. "Funny things do happen, though.
Our rocks have been known to jump out and hit cars
driven by Yanks, and our trees do lean
sometimes into their right-of-way.
But you'll be okay.
Just keep the center line out *your* window.
If it shows up out your wife's, it's a nuisance."

Four days later we returned the car
without a scratch, having achieved some level of comfort
with oddities such as laybys, round-abouts, dual carriageways,
even narrow roads with high rock walls for shoulders.
In truth, though, we caught our breath each time
a car sailed over the rise ahead
and we watched it coming at us lickety-split
with no one sitting where the driver ought to sit.

VI

Partridge
(after Ovid)

Daedalus — on wings of wax and feathers.
Wings, too, for high flying Icarus.
Wax in sun's heat — feathers loosen.
Icarus — a plunge from sky to ocean.
Daedalus, a father no longer, curses his skill.
Feathers dot the water where Icarus fell.

As Daedalus made a tomb to bury the boy,
a partridge, sounding overjoyed,
popped its head from a nearby ditch,
clapped its wings, and screeched *k-SHEEE-ritch*!
keep keep k-SHEEE-ritch! At the time
that partridge was the only one of its kind;
nobody had seen anything like it before.
To Daedalus, the bird was a stern reproach.
His sister, knowing Daedalus's renown
as an inventor, had sent her twelve-year-old son
for instruction. Clearly the boy had a fertile mind.
Observing the backbone of a fish, he had notched an iron
blade with teeth, inventing the saw.
Likewise, he is the first to have thought
of joining two metal arms in such a way
that, if their points remain the same
distance apart and one stands still, the other
will describe a circle around it. Utterly
beside himself with jealousy, Daedalus
greeted the boy by hurling him down
from the walls of Athena's city,
then told everyone the boy fell accidentally.

But Athena, patron of the ingenious, caught Partridge
(that was the boy's name) as he fell and changed
him into a bird, clothing him with feathers
in mid-air. Now his old quickness of wit occurs
as swiftness of wing and foot. Even so,
the bird refuses ever to soar
or build its nest up high on a limb
or point of rock. Instead, it makes its home
on the ground and lays its eggs in hedgerows —
remembering the fall long ago.

The First Fire
(a Cherokee myth)

In the beginning there was no fire
and the world was cold, until the Thunders
sent lightning to put fire in the bottom of a hollow sycamore
that stood on an island in a Blue Ridge lake.
The animals knew the fire was there —
they could see the smoke — but because of the water,
they couldn't get to it. So they held a council.
This was a long time ago, before there were any people.

The council was noisy; every animal
that could fly or swim wanted to go for the fire.
The Raven, always pleased with himself,
stretched out his wings to draw attention,
and because he was so strong and daring,
the others thought he could surely do the job.
He flew high over the water, doing a tumble
to let his white feathers sparkle in the sun,
and alighted on the sycamore. But while he sat there
wondering what to do, the heat scorched
his white feathers. He grew alarmed and flew back
now black all over and without any fire.
Then there was talk among the owls, who looked grave,
and everyone turned to the Hoot Owl.
But when he got to the blazing tree, the smoke
nearly blinded him, and ashes drafting upwards
made white rings around his eyes.
He had to wait for nighttime to fly back,
sunlight hurting his eyes. And despite much rubbing
he never got rid of the white rings.

All the birds were nervous now,
so the Possum strutted up and said he would go.
Always proud of his good looks —

much handsomer than a fox, he told himself often —
the possum set off swimming strongly,
swishing his big bushy tail like a paddle.
At the base of the tree he found a crack
in the trunk, but before he could reach in,
a gust of wind blew out sparks
that set his wonderful tail on fire.
Quickly he jumped in the lake, but swam home slowly.
To this day his tail is hairless;
and embarrassed, he slinks around only at night.

It hadn't gone well for animals that fly or walk,
so the great Coppersnake raised his head high in the air
and flicked his tongue. He got his name
from his color, and is called *the climber*.
He slithered across the lake, only his head above water,
and climbed the tree as the coppersnake always does,
but when he put his head down the hole,
smoke choked him and he fell in.
Before he could climb back out he was burned all over.
Now he is known as the great Blacksnake.

Still no fire, and the world was still cold,
but now all the animals had some excuse
for not going, because they were afraid to venture
near the burning sycamore, until at last
the little Water Spider said she would go.
This is not the water spider that looks like a mosquito,
but the other one, with black downy hair
and red stripes on her body, that can run on top of the water
or dive down deep. She would have no trouble
getting to the island. The question was:
How could she bring back the fire?
"I'll manage," she said, and struck out across the lake
and through the grass to the burning tree.
There, as if born for the work, she spun
a thread from her body, wove a basket,

and in it cradled a tiny coal of fire.
Then she spun another thread to fasten the basket
on her back and set out across the lake
with a happy heart. The other animals, shivering,
waited for her on tiptoes. It was hard going,
and when she got back she was so tired
she barely noticed how joyful the animals were
at her return with her warm little burden.

A Savage Response:
the Council of the Iroquois Confederation
to the College of William and Mary
(1744)

Sirs, you have invited us
to send you twelve of our sons
for what you style a proper education.
We know that you highly esteem the kind
of learning taught in colleges, and that
the maintenance of our young men
would be very expensive to you.
We are convinc'd, therefore, that you mean
to do us good by your proposal;
and we thank you heartily. But you,
who are wise, must know that different nations
have different conceptions of things. You will
therefore not take it amiss if our ideas
of this kind of education differ from yours.
We have had some experience of it.
Several of our young people were formerly
brought up at colleges of the northern provinces.
They were instructed in all your sciences,
but when they came back to us they were
bad runners, ignorant of every means
of living in the woods, unable to bear
either cold or hunger; knew neither how to
build a cabin, take a deer, or kill an enemy,
spoke our language imperfectly, were therefore
neither fit for hunters, warriors, nor counselors.
They were in plain truth good for nothing at all.

We are, however, not the less obliged
by your kind offer, though we decline it;
and, to show our grateful sense of it,
if the Gentlemen of Virginia will send us
a dozen of their sons, we will take care
of their education, instruct them in all
we know, and make men of them.

Last Words of Nanye'hi,
Beloved Woman of the Cherokees,
to the Cherokee Council
(MAY 2, 1817)

Assembled Chiefs, the women before you
bring greetings from one now too old to travel.

Long ago our Cherokee lands were vast,
but treaties parting with land for paltry sums
have reduced our territory to the western Blue Ridge.
Although we never thought of land as a thing
to buy or sell, we haven't felt it our duty
to advise you till now, when white people want this tract, too —
all that is left us. Now our duty as mothers drives us:
Do not put your hands to the white man's paper,
do not part with our last bit of land.
That would be like destroying your mothers.

Beloved head men of the Cherokee Nation,
let me find words for your own best thoughts.
For us, the territory over the Mississippi
is a faceless place. Our blood and bones are not there;
it is barren ground for our spirit. How unlike
our Blue Ridge home! These mountains were made for us —
our Promised Land, fruitful for ourselves, our children,
and all the children to come.

Remember the story of strawberries told by the elders —
how the first man and woman quarreled, and the woman
left her husband and started off toward the morning Sun.
Her husband followed, grieving, but she kept steadily on
and never looked back. The Sun, knowing their need
for one another, took pity and caused a bush
of the plumpest blueberries to spring up on a ridge she crossed,
but she passed by without paying them any mind.
Then in a ravine the Sun put a tangle of bright blackberries,
but these as well she refused to notice. Then suddenly
in a high meadow she saw a patch of large ripe strawberries.
Stooping to gather a few to eat, she chanced
to turn her face toward home. At once the memory
of her husband came back to her and she found herself
unable to go on. The longer she waited
the stronger grew her desire for her husband.
At last she picked a bunch of the finest berries
and started back to give him a taste.
These were the first strawberries ever seen!
And they token how the mountains fill our needs.

Beloved chiefs, in these mountains we raised
all of you, and now tend your children.
When I close my eyes, I see
smiling babies tumbling from the clouds
into the arms of their mothers, and as soon as
one child is raised, we find others in our arms.
It should go on like that forever.

The Americans know the land is ours; otherwise
they would not offer us money for it. And our Father,
the President, will not allow his white children
to steal away our country. It is beyond belief!
So this is what you must do: enlarge your farms,
plant more corn and squash and cotton,
all for your growing children and the ones to come
in the bright days ahead.

Only Yonaguska
(QUALLA BOUNDARY, FALL 1836)

"You stand *here*," he said to the woman,
  pointing to a place near the council house.
"You stand *there*," he said to her husband,
  pointing to a place a little way off toward the river.

Like the bugling of elks in the meadow,
Yonaguska's thoughts rang in his mind.

"My friends," he said to the fifty families
who followed him, "the whites want us gone from here.
They lust for these mountains that were made for us
when the land first rose from the water."

Like lightning licking at mountain ridges,
land-lusting whites, he knew, lurked all around them.

"Many of our Cherokee brothers and sisters feed
their hearts on fantasies. A few, despairing of a fight,
signed a treaty selling the lands of the Cherokee Nation
and promising all will move west."

Like a blood-red sunset over Oklahoma prairies,
the killing of those traitors spread before his mind.

"Most of our people are outraged by such betrayal.
They do not want to leave the land of our ancestors,
and still hope the Americans — their leaders and laws —
will let them stay here, a Nation within a nation."

Like a rabbit in the talons of an eagle, Chief John Ross,
he knew, was fast in the clutches of President Jackson.

"That is a foolish hope. I am taller
than other Cherokees, and see farther in both directions.
In the past, what have the Americans done
but break their treaties and burn our crops and towns."

Like doves in the field whistling up at a footfall,
his family had run to the hills from Rutherford's raiders.

"And in the future they will hold to the last treaty
because it satisfies their greed for the land of the Nation.
They will round us up at gunpoint and drive us
to the west, the land of the dead."

Like a herd of cattle — hungry, heart-sore, sick —
his people he saw stumbling along the trail.

"But I will not be on that trail. The Treaty of 1819 said,
if the head of a household withdraws from the Nation
and becomes a citizen of the United States, he gains title
to a square mile of land and the protection of American laws."

Like a hunter lost, then spotting a path he can follow,
he had listened as the agent outlined Article 2.

"I am told Andrew Jackson let the article stand
only because he knew few Cherokees would renounce
the Cherokee Nation. *Of them all*, Jackson said,
only Yonaguska might see the opportunity here."

Just as an oak is an oak whatever it is called,
Yonaguska was Cherokee whatever they called him.

"I have papers from the Americans for my land,
 but the land itself will protect us from their aggression.
 In this stretch of rocky hills we are safer
 than we could ever be on land white men thought profitable."

Like the Garden of Eden, his home, Kituhwa,
was for Cherokees the place of creation for all living things.

"So, my friends, I say: if you wish to stay here with me
 in this sacred place, and not be cast out,
 follow me across the line between Ela and her husband, John Atsi."
 Some laughing, others solemn, all followed him.

Like canoeists on a stretch of white-water in rough weather,
his people he saw tossed down the decades, but never crushed.

Apples, Junaluska, Dancing

Next time you're in Snowbird country, notice
the apple trees shading the seven stones marking
Junaluska's grave. The trees are named for him,

Junaluska, and bear "a magnificent apple,"
says the *Magazine of Horticulture*, 1857.
"Quality, the best"— yet were lost to growers

a hundred years till apple hunter Tom Brown
found an old tree, salvaging a heritage, and revived
the story of the Cherokee who outwitted the Red Stick Creeks

at Horseshoe Bend down in Alabama,
giving Andrew Jackson a victory and prompting his vow
in pigeon Indian, "as long as the sun shines

and the grass grows, there shall be friendship between us,
and the feet of the Cherokee shall be toward the east" — a vow flouted
when, as President, he fostered the Trail of Tears

on which Junaluska and fifteen thousand others
trudged to Oklahoma, many dying on the way.
But a year later Junaluska stretched his legs

back to North Carolina, where he was made a citizen
"for military services" and awarded a farm
in the Snowbird region of Graham County.

It won't hurt you to hear how he developed the apple
with his wife, the fine farmer Nicie. Year after year,
grafting scion wood to rootstock for the bite he liked,

they worked their way, planting trees
on mountainside clearings above the line where killing frosts
pool in the valleys in early spring

(soil losing heat faster than air over long nights),
adding bee hives for sure pollination, thinning young apples
to limit limb breakage and allow larger fruit.

The Junaluska, not a beauty (dull greenish skin
splotched with russet), stops you cold with its taste:
spicy rich, so juicy it waters your thirst.

Late October, when hardwoods light up the Snowbird Mountains,
folks flocked to his farm for apples and apple blossom honey.
Nor can it do you harm to hear how every fall

he celebrated the harvest with dances, men and women
circling heaped baskets to the beat of drums and rattles,
the autumn air zesty with apple tang.

VII

Signs

At the Parkway overlook a Florida car
screeched to a halt, and the driver called out to me:
"Hey buddy, where's Asheville?"

                                   "Up the Parkway
north about thirty miles."

                                   "No, I mean,
what state's it in?"

                              "Last I heard it was North Carolina."

"A hell of a note! I'm supposed to be in Tennessee —
heading into Knoxville, Tennessee. No reason
in the world why I'm in North Carolina. Musta made
a wrong turn someplace."

      "Not hard to do in these mountains."

"Damn! Drive all day, sun in your face,
kids driving you crazy, wife ready to kill you!
How do I get to Tennessee?"

"North a couple of miles — *up that way* — a road
cuts off to the Interstate. Quickest way to Knoxville.
Just follow the big green signs. You can't go wrong."

"Thanks!" he called back, squealing his wheels
down the Parkway south.

           I threw up a hand to stop him,
but he was gone.

"Goodness!" my wife said. "Poor man!
Must be that attention disorder thing — what
do you call it?"

"Or it could be Spirit People offering up a sign.
Cherokees say Spirit People inhabit these high mountains —
kind gentle souls, visible or invisible as they choose,
always looking for ways to help you out."

"I don't see how getting lost could help anybody."

"Maybe it's a sign for us: *Caution.
Navigate With Care.*"

"I didn't know you were joking!"

"This is Cherokee country. Don't you feel
their eyes on us from the woods? To them these mountains
were a nest made by a giant buzzard just for
the Cherokee people. And it was a good place to live —
the hills and streams alive with generous spirits.
But a nor'easter blew through called Manifest Destiny
and scattered them toward the west. At the time
my great-grandmother's people were among the fewer
than a thousand Cherokees to weather the storm
up here in the old homelands."

"I'm feeling vibrations
from her now, I think."

"Our Florida friend
twisting down the Parkway south — have you thought
where he'll come out?"

"Why, at Cherokee,
the Indian village. The Parkway ends there,
dumps you off like a big slide board
right at the edge of town."

"He has no clue
what brought him to North Carolina, but his problems
cry out for help. Maybe he was drawn here,
like a flower turning toward the sun for the light it needs.
In Cherokee, maybe he happens on the right old-timers,
who take him to a bend in the Oconaluftee where he looks up-stream
while facing east, and instruct him how to dip
in the cold running water, letting his mind *play* on the seven directions.
First, the compass points: west, where death resides;
north, the origin of troubles; south, the seat of peace;
and east — where he looks — the direction of triumph.
Then down to the earth, our mother, and up to the sky,
our father. Then into the center of himself.
That's what Cherokees call *going to water* —
an ancient healing ceremony where you find yourself
by losing yourself in the rhythms of nature.
It ends with a prayer to the river — the *Long Man* —
for the eyes of a hawk in finding your path,
and the speed of a deer in following it."

"*Let his mind play on . . .*
I like that. It catches — well, what? — the *playfulness* of meditation,
even on deep things. And I love their ceremony —
all but the cold water part."

"You'd please the Cherokees, my love. They're well disposed,
much of the time, toward those of us they still think of
as boat people."

The Scottish Thistle, So Called

(a Mediterranean native)

This thistle has a right to be put out with people.
Were the plant like us, it would have to grapple

with a crisis of identity. In fact it rarely
grows in the land of bagpipes and kilts. (In Pitlockery

they had to *plant* one for tourists to photograph.)
Legend has it that a tenth century gaffe

by Danish raiders made the thistle the shamrock of Scotland.
In a midnight raid on the Scottish king's castle, the band

stripped naked to swim the moat and jumped, all a-bristle,
into a ditch pumped dry and filled with thistles.

Shrieks roused the guard, and the land was spared
rape and pillage. Fine for people — but look how the affair

skewed things for thistles. Suppose *you* were a native of Greece.
How would you like it if people never would cease

calling you Scotty? And what about having your fame
rest on your least attractive feature? You've a stately frame

with crimson crown, and you mature quite quickly.
Stickers? — It's almost incidental that you're a bit prickly.

Blue Wildflowers

A group of women
moves beside the stream in morning mist,
their voices rising and falling,
but whether in song, lamentation, or battle chant
you couldn't say. On their shoulders
are poles with ends made heavy
by what could be stones chipped
as hoe blades, ax heads, spear points.
Some have bundles strapped on their back.
Ahead of them
a patch of wildflowers takes shape in the shifting mist,
maybe blue wood asters
since they stand erect and exude a bluish luster.
The women move resolutely toward the patch,
perhaps intent on nourishing a cherished site
by digging in scraps of nutrients,
perhaps intent on destroying a spot
defiled by rape or killing or other sacrilege
by hacking down all markings of the place,
or it could be to take a moment's joy
in the shrouded beauty as they make their journey.

Autumn Scene with Hound

October's yellow light
from a high wispy sky.
Warm bench
snug by shrubs.
Nothing stirs.
For one with thoughts to think,
a stillness bright with purpose

until a hound rounds the house
and lopes in loopy frolic
over gray grass,
woofing at squirrels and robins
and nothing at all,
in the frantic way
of hounds off scent.

Into the Wild

I'm pulled in by bluets where the trail
greets the woods, dragged along by sunbeams
on tangled brambles where a lily
dangles from its stalk, yellow petals

flaming out to orange and curving back
till tips touch like a winter cap with flaps
folded up for summer — then swish, swish, crack
on the ridge just above me. I know what it is.

Not deer, who amble quietly;
nor people, who'd be down here on the trail.
A quarter mile back persimmon bark showed claw marks
where a bear climbed for fruit.

The bear on the ridge lumbers along
heedless of me, the breeze blowing my way,
then seems to wander over the ridge
and down the other side as the crack of stepped-on sticks,

the swish of brushed branches fade away.
I go along to the overlook I came to see
and start back musing on persimmons —
an Indian name, Algonquian, I think,

in a genus called *fruit of the gods* in Latin,
which fits only after bitter balls ripen to sweetness
at fall's first frost. Then a sharp grunt
from the ridge. I stop mid-step.

The bear had only paused at some berries or acorns,
and now I am the one upwind.
On hind legs — black against the trees —
he sniffs the breeze and spots me.

Dropping to all fours, he lunges a step my way,
snuffling and slapping the ground with a paw.
I back slowly away not to crowd him, wondering
how best to fight back should he do more than bluff.

Bluffing, too, I yell "Hey!"
and wave my arms. The bear sits back.
I'm not new, he's seen my kind before,
and, his nose telling him I carry no food,

he wheels and gallops off through the trees.
"Brother, go well," I call once my heart
starts beating again. His fading sound is like
a wind rustling the mountain fastness.

Visitations

Walking out from camp one morning,
I thought of going back to read
until I came to a trail I'd never hiked,
up to a lodge abandoned decades ago
that park rangers told me about. A hard hike,
they said, but worth it if old things grab you.

They weren't kidding about the hike.
The trail was level into the trees,
then turned up at once with an incline so steep
it had to be cut at angles across the mountain side,
with sharp switchbacks like a sailboat
tacking across the wind.

Not a hiking trail at all,
it had been cut as an ox-cart path,
so an ox with handler out front could haul people up
in a narrow two-wheeled cart — a nail-biter
with the path in good shape; impossible now.

Tumbled rocks and fallen trees
littered the path in places, and its crumbling edges
soon looked down on treetops hundreds of feet below —
a sight that made me dizzy. In other places
low limbs and bushes closed in like walls
of a windowless room. I knew a river
glinted in the valley, but I couldn't see it.
I knew ridges fell away to the horizon,
some with shining rock faces where falcons nest,
but I saw only the leaves and needles in my face.

Eyes watery and stinging, I found myself
thinking again of turning back — to hell with old lodges!
But as I muttered, the path got less steep and slowly
leveled out. I had made it to the summit.

The lodge, its lumber milled from trees whose place
it took, was caving in. A two-story section
that housed the guest rooms lacked a corner of its roof.
And years ago wind uprooted an oak
that fell through the roof of the single-story dining hall.
I had climbed to see a ruin.

But a walk around suggested its grand past.
Trees still thinned out where builders
had opened a view of ridges rolling away
as far as eye could see —
green to purple to smoky gray —
a view worth the cart ride up.
And I could close my eyes and see
the dining hall from photos on the wall
of the ranger station: guests enjoying dinner
in the glow of candle-lit chandeliers
before a huge stone fireplace. I found myself
imagining those men and women who rode an ox-cart up
to escape the summer heat wearing ties and jackets,
high collars and long skirts that muffled
cool breezes they hoped to enjoy. Yet they
kept coming back till the crash of '29.

On a side wall I spotted some hiker's scrawl:
Visitation is only by ghosts.
He was about right. He and I
had ventured up, but the uninviting trail
would bring few hikers by
before the decaying pile gave back to the mountain
its borrowed wood and stone — its power
to quicken the mind's eye gone forever.
I might have earned a distinction today:
last person to see the old place
while two boards hung together.

Monarchs

I had thought the Grand Canyon something. But butterflies
that find the high fir forests of central Mexico
from as far away as Hudson Bay — how do they know
the place when no one of them completes
the yearly round-trip? And why do they bother? No other
butterfly migrates on that scale. Besides which, *how?*
One-way could be five thousand miles, weather foul
some of the time most likely — sleet? blustering
wind on butterfly wing? Still, they manage.
Moving northward in the spring, mating
along the way, they leave eggs anticipating
a circuit the species perfects. At the edge
of our meadow in June milkweed flickers flames
as egg-heavy females swirl and light, frantic, then calm.